Alison,

writ

much

love,

Laure

"Some few lucky people find the missing piece of themselves in the eyes of another, becoming together the best of God's creations. This tender book is an instant classic. It compellingly describes the love between two special people, inspiring us all to follow their example."

Val Halamandaris
President, National Association
for Home Care and Hospice

"There are very few people who have been gifted with the genius of spirit and intellect, have been touched by the ecstasy of complete and eternal love, and are so talented as writers that their prose and poetry can elicit magic from the hearts of others. Lance Secretan is one such individual. His ability to capture the beauty of his love for his soul mate, Tricia, is sublime. And his courage to share his heartfelt feelings with a world that so desperately needs to be reminded of the power of love is a wondrous gift for all of us. *A Love Story* will make you laugh and it will make you cry, and in the end, you will be a better person for it. You will realize that if the Universe can bless us with such an amazing sensual and spiritual love, there is definitely hope for us to rise above our challenges to a sustainable future."

James A. Cusumano, PhD
Author of *Life Is Beautiful: 12 Universal Rules*

"No matter where you are in life and love, you will be moved by Lance and Tricia's love story. This book is for anyone who has ever loved, who wants to love, or who wants to be inspired in their love relationship. Good things truly do come in small packages, as Lance Secretan opens another door to his heart and soul by sharing vignettes from the most profound love relationship of his life. A series of true stories that may make you cry, laugh, or contemplate, this book will inspire you and fill you with hope and the deep knowledge that true soul-love never dies."

Nancy J. Wood, Vancouver Island, British Columbia

"*A Love Story* is a witty, intimate look at two people who love each other. Secretan has interspersed stories with poems and quotes, and this gives a vitality to his narrative. The poem "Zen River," for instance, reaches out to make you think. The stories on how Lance courted Trish, and then how she showed her love and friendship are funny, serious, and sexy. Wait until you read about the fur coat! I read through the book once in an evening, and then reread many of the stories and poems. I suspect that most readers will do the same."

Bob Chernow, former Vice Chair,
World Future Society

"*A Love Story* is a beautiful journey into the heart and mind of a great leader."

Coach Dave Buck, CEO, CoachVille

"In his newest offering, *A Love Story*, Lance Secretan shares a moving account of his astounding relationship with the love of his life, Tricia. It is a beautiful collection of original poetry and personal stories woven together to create a powerful ode to love. From a chance meeting on the ski slopes, the two souls came together with a love that grew stronger each year and continues to endure. In a beautifully open and authentic voice, Lance invites us into a deeper contemplation of the myriad of ways love is expressed in our lives. After reading this book, you will be inspired to take up the metaphoric pen and draft your own love story. In our fast-paced, sound-bite world, this is surely the siren call for deeper connection."

Megan Hoernke, author and coach, Ontario, Canada

"My life has been blessed beyond words by the friendship of Lance and Tricia Secretan. Thank you, Lance, for *A Love Story*, for it allows me to enter into the intimate sacred partnership that touched me so deeply. To be able to hold this book in my hands and be reminded of the relationship that inspired me and all who witnessed it is a beautiful gift. The book is sure to inspire all who will read your loving, poetic account of a most precious love story indeed."

Christine Smith, Calgary, Alberta

A Love Story

An Intensely Personal Memoir

LANCE SECRETAN

Library and Archives Canada Cataloguing in Publication

Secretan, Lance H. K., author

A love story : an intensely personal memoir / Lance H.K. Secretan.

ISBN 978-0-9865654-1-0 (bound)

1. Secretan, Lance H. K--Anecdotes. 2. Secretan, Patricia--Anecdotes.
3. Love--Anecdotes. 4. Business consultants--Anecdotes. I. Title.

HD69.C6S43 2015   658.40092'2   C2015-907072-4

Published by the Secretan Center Inc.
Caledon, Ontario, Canada

Edited by: Simone Gabbay, simonegabbay.com
Cover illustrations: David Rankin, davidrankineart.com
Cover design: Ewa Henry
Text design: Heidy Lawrance, WeMakeBooks.ca
Author's cover photo courtesy of Sally Wright

Printed in Canada

If you would like to contact the author to order his books, videos, DVDs, or CDs, or to arrange a public speaking engagement, please do so at the following coordinates:

Dr. Lance H. K. Secretan
The Secretan Center Inc.
Web Site: www.secretan.com
E-mail: info@secretan.com

To everyone who yearns for true love,

to those who have found it,

and to those who are rediscovering it.

Love is like a friendship caught on fire. In the beginning a flame, very pretty, often hot and fierce, but still only light and flickering. As love grows older, our hearts mature and our love becomes as coals, deep-burning and unquenchable.

—Bruce Lee

Table of Contents

Preface

*I*n between the 15 business books I have written over the last 40 years, I have been writing (but rarely publishing) poetry. I have sneaked a couple of poems into those books, but they were usually gently and surreptitiously placed within the larger text.

Poetry is a window into the soul. Poetry is emotion recalled with serenity. We read poetry with our hearts more than our eyes. People tend to write poetry about things for which they have great passion. As Robert Frost said, "Poetry is when emotion has found its thought and the thought has found words." My private attempts to play with words this way have centered around my love for Tricia—the center of my universe— or my curiosity about the wonders of life and our little

planet and the rest of the cosmos. It has been my
cathartic way to connect my soul to paper. And for
that purpose, poetry is much more efficient than prose.
Poetry enhances the language, somehow making it richer
than prose constructed from the same words. For me,
poetry has a way of capturing and suspending life's
magical moments, like the beauty of a flower preserved
and suspended in amber.

Poets elicit the sweet sensuality of language from
the ether to the forefront of our senses with alliteration
and rhyme, while only hinting at the complexity that lies
behind the craftily assembled words. Poetry, to the poet
and to the reader, represents a voice from a deeper place
than even the finest prose; if the memo or the email
emanates from the personality, poetry must surely be
the voice of the soul.

This is a very personal book. It is, as the book's
title suggests, a love story—and as Ben Hecht points
out, "Love is the magician that pulls man out of his
own hat." I have chosen some highlights of the remarkable journey that has been the magic of Tricia's and my

love story and first described them in prose and tied a ribbon at the end of each story with a poem that was written, usually in that moment and at that time, over the last 30 years.

It is a small book about a big subject—a love story as big as the Universe. I hope that it inspires you and that you will love reading it as much as I have loved living it.

Ode to Belles-Lettres

The words are speaking with my mind
In silent dialogue
An intellectual anodyne
That's oiling ev'ry cog.
A hundred thousand silent sounds
Reposing in my brain
Ensuring that the thoughts they found
Won't be the same again.

Do some great writers comprehend
When paper meets their ink
Their words turn strangers into friends
More often than they think?
And then these friendships when they're shared
Elaborate our loves and fears
Revealing how we dared and cared
To speak the truth through tears.

A Love Story

Between two covers dance rich sounds
Relieving my distress,
Sowing seeds on fertile grounds
That nourish consciousness.
The tilled soil of my cognition
Enriched so by the greats
Turns seeds of thought to fruition
Across my mind's estate.

Once Upon a Time...

...**there** was a beautiful young woman sharing lunch with three of her girlfriends. On this crisp winter's day, the four friends sat in the corner lounge of the Four Seasons Hotel in Toronto, surveying the flow of humanity through the vaulted glass windows. Tricia, being freshly divorced, reflected on her new independence. Her friends urged her to start dating, but she said, "No way!" Then, to add emphasis, she went on, "Men? I'm done! Done, done! I mean DONE."

But one of the young women persisted. "Let's play a game. Why don't you create a list of all the attributes that you would wish for in your *perfect man?*"

Reluctantly, Tricia agreed, and began compiling a list. It quickly grew. It had all the typical attributes: handsome, single, fit, athletic, intelligent, great sense of humor, no emotional baggage, good dancer, good manners, good taste, and more. Looking at the list, long and demanding though it was, Tricia feared that, even so, there might be a candidate who would fit all these criteria. So she decided to raise the bar, and throw in some hurdles.

"He needs to be a man who will not roll his eyes if I bring him a bouquet of flowers," she said. Feeling quite pleased with this deflective strategy, she piled it on. "He needs to belong to my local, member-only ski club," she said, knowing full well that it was a family club with few, if any, single members.

Tricia's friends threw up their hands in defeat.

Soon after, as Tricia skied down one of the runs at her ski club, she caught an edge and fell over. Lance had joined the club three weeks earlier and, coming across Tricia lying in the snow, he helped her to her feet. He blew the snow out of her ear, and fell in love.

Shortly after Tricia and Lance's first date at her ski chalet,[1] Tricia arrived at Lance's home for dinner carrying a bouquet of flowers, which also contained a teddy bear and a Mickey Mouse watch. No eyes rolled. An eternal union was forged.

[1]See the next story

No Thoroughfare

Oh, I'm in trouble...

The sign across my heart
Was clear for all to see
It said "no thoroughfare";
I meant it seriously.
My mind placed the sign there
But my heart took it down.
A pixie cast her spell—
Made me a helpless clown.

The Ski Chalet

*T*ricia's mom has lent her ski chalet to Tricia so that she can invite her sales team—all women —for a social weekend. On the spur of the moment, Tricia has invited me over to join them all for dinner. Our first date!

We are both like teenagers, giddy with excitement and anticipation. Tricia's sales team is not sure what to make of all this—it seems to them that we are an event within an event. They are a group of clucking hens, very protective of Tricia, not wanting her to fall for some guy who picked her up on the ski hill. So they take turns to exit the kitchen, where they are washing and drying dishes, to provide unsolicited chaperone services to ensure, in their minds, that everything is under control.

In between these ladies' interventions, I am trying
to steal a first kiss. But it feels a bit like trying to run
across an interstate highway during rush hour.

Finally, I succeed, in between chaperone visits—
a sort of staccato victory.

The kiss!

My heart is racing—I am falling for this Angel
—I need oxygen! Her kisses are like honey and fire—
a magical message told through the lips.

Tricia and I are sitting on the sofa in front of a
large picture window. The sales team in the kitchen,
unbeknownst to us, is able to monitor what we think
is our secret in the reflective glass. *The kiss* may have
been historic for Tricia and me, but when witnessed
in the reflection of the picture window, it was far
from covert and it prompted an immediate evacuation
of the kitchen.

This transforms the temporary team of chaperones
into a permanent one. If they were all Navy SEALs
with the two of us centered in the cross wires of

their M4 rifles, we could not be more encircled. But for them, it is too late; *the kiss*, our first ever, is now ours to treasure—forever.

How do I feel now? Jiddu Krishnamurti described it well: "The moment you have in your heart this extraordinary thing called love and feel the depth, the delight, the ecstasy of it, you will discover that for you the world is transformed."

The Kiss

Savor each kiss
With the zest of a man
Not destined to see
Another day pass.
Thus every day
Must on its own stand
In case it might be
Your love's very last.

A Cabin in the Woods

I tell Tricia there is a sign above my heart that says, "No thoroughfare."

This comes from a poem by Herbert Simpson:

> *Across the gateway of my heart*
> *I wrote "No thoroughfare,"*
> *But love came laughing by, and cried,*
> *"I enter everywhere."*

I tell her, "I am aware that I am falling in love, but I have made a commitment to myself that I am going to remain single." It's not that I am afraid that I might lead her on, or that I might let her down; it's more about me—I feel like a drug addict, and my pusher is about to claim my soul. If I don't resist, I will fall into this sublime trap.

One Sunday afternoon, as Tricia and I are mountain-biking on the quiet country roads, we stop for a moment in the opening of a driveway. It winds its way through a forest to the edge of a cliff that hangs 400 feet above a vast expanse of emptiness—800 acres of pristine wilderness. The breathtaking views reach into forever. The property seems deserted, so we lean our bikes against a tree and quietly merge into the panorama. A small log cabin, assembled from old-growth western cedar, comes into view. We stand at the cliff's edge in silent awe, drinking in the breathtaking views of this, the first United Nations biosphere, devoid of a single man-made light or human mark.

I fall in love again—this time with the prospect of the monastic experience I am yearning for. I am a writer. I ache to live in a log cabin in the woods, with a beer fridge by my bedside, unencumbered by humans who need something from me.

I call a realtor friend and ask him to enquire about the property and whether it is for sale. He tells me that it was just put on the market but has not yet been listed and therefore, for the time being, has no public profile. I ask him to arrange a meeting with the owner, which he does for the following day.

When Tricia and I meet the owner, she tells us that this was a country cottage belonging to her mother, who has just died. She says that she also owns another cottage in Ontario's northern lake district. She tells me she can't decide which of the two cottages to keep. I make the decision easy for her—I offer to buy this one, for the asking price—on the spot, and she accepts.

After I move in, I discover that the cottage has been rarely inhabited—I vacuum out six bags of cobwebs. The windows are "sealed" with sisal rope, which, over many years of neglect, has disintegrated into dust. Water is rising from the ground and seeping into the log walls. Freshwater springs are bubbling all around the property, and every kind of wild thing is roaming around, having grown accustomed to the primal environment. It is exactly what I need right now—silent, isolated, primitive, and seamlessly woven into nature.

Over the summer, Tricia helps me to move in and we spend a lot of time there together. Tricia helps me to decorate, buy furniture, and create a cozy home. As winter approaches, Tricia is spending more time in the cabin in the woods than in her own home. The camel has its nose in the tent.

Burlesque in the Woods

Descending from the canopy
It rested at my feet,
The woodland's verdant panoply,
Its cycle now complete.

A sylvan striptease so demure,
Discarding gold and brown,
Majestic boughs spill their allure
As carpets on the ground.

Emerald was the apogee
That now is steely-blue.
The woods must rest awhile, you see,
Before their next debut.

Perfection

*T*his woman is incredible!

She is beautiful. She has blonde hair and large brown eyes so deep they make the Mariana Trench look like a puddle. Van Morrison's melody plays in my head: "Our hearts a thumpin' and you, My brown-eyed girl, You're my brown-eyed girl."

She is an athlete, sensual, exciting, beautifully proportioned, muscle-toned, slim, and gorgeously contoured. Her skin is flawless except for a mole at the top of her décolletage. And who would call that a flaw? I long to kiss it for infinity.

Tricia's laugh is completely infectious and drizzled with joy, like the innocence and delight found in the spontaneity and transparency of a child's laughter. She savors the moment and shares it with all. Hearing

Tricia's laugh makes my soul smile—nothing else brings me greater joy. Her laugh is the sunshine in the house.

And she is whip-smart, and endlessly funny. When Coco Chanel observed, "A girl should be two things: classy and fabulous," she must have been thinking of Tricia as her prototype.

But what is on the outside pales in comparison to what is inside, and what is outside is amplified by what is inside. What would be simple beauty in another becomes mega-beauty with Tricia because her soul radiates and illuminates—not only her, but all those around her.

I often tell Tricia how beautiful she is, and she smiles—Wow! That Smile!—and each time she remarks coyly, "You're silly! That's just because you love me." Even if that's true, it doesn't explain why Tricia turns the heads of strangers when they enter her orbit. Sometimes I amuse myself by dropping half a pace behind Tricia, watching how the world reacts to her. Is it just because they love her too?

You don't learn this beauty—it comes from a deep place. There are no courses where one learns to cause others to swoon. This kind of beauty is God's work.

I decide to call her "Beautiful," because she is.

"Can I make you a coffee, Beautiful?"

The Mansion of My Mind

In the mansion of my mind
Your laughter graces every room
And the flowers in my garden strain
To share their smiles with the moon

Lovers

The air at the summit is rare
Offering Nirvana
To a beautiful pair
Implanting our banner
To celebrate life—
My Dear.

My fantasies waltz in the love
That dances in your eyes
My hand is in your glove
And my heart mesmerized—
My Love.

The climax is our terrain
But our lips are sealed as we rest,
For how can we impart
The view from the crest—
Sweetheart?

Hands

I notice that Tricia has beautiful hands. Beautifully manicured, they are remarkably small and yet strong. She decorates them with the diamonds she has earned from being the country's number one sales director for Mary Kay. Like Michelangelo's "Creation of Adam," Tricia's hands draw your attention—they mesmerize me, and I can't stop looking at them.

Tricia is very tactile—thank goodness—and when her hand reaches for mine, a billion-megawatt switch is thrown in my body and electricity charges my entire being. Never has the touch of a hand contained this power for me.

If Tricia rubs my head, I am in ecstasy. If she massages the knots in my neck, I moan with delight. I realize that true love reciprocates and so I offer to do the same for her. I run my hands through her hair—this generates rapture even greater than that I feel when skiing in freshly fallen, untracked, chest-high powder. My hand massages the nape of her neck, where her hair ends in a small V, and it is the most delicious place to kiss—felt but unseen for Tricia. I reason that kissing the nape of her neck and massaging it with my hand at the same time, adds to the therapeutic effect—although I'm not sure if I mean for me or for her—and perhaps it's both. I love this girl, "A thousand kisses deep," as Leonard Cohen has written.

Her hands in mine, brushing my cheek, offering a high five or a fist bump, taking my arm, welcoming me home, pointing the way, lighting a candle, stroking, hugging, turning out the lights—a gentle touch that no other can match. The touch of a lover's hand.

Hands

Rest from your toils
A minute or two,
And roll your frayed
Sleeves up your wrist;
The tools that you see
In front of you
Are two of the
Best that exist.

How many years
Would mankind require
To invent a
Device so fine?
The ides of never
Could not inspire
Such a flawless,
Divine Design.

The hand weaves threads
Into tapestry,
And creates joy
With a gentle stroke,
Teases colors
Into artistry,
And plants acorns
For future oaks.

Would an artist
Or any draughtsman,
The most gifted
Or magic of men,
Maintain the panache
Of the craftsman
If his hands were
Not part of him?

When Beethoven
Pondered these lessons,
His great music
Swept through the lands—
Testimony to
The quintessence,
Of man and his
Beautiful hands

How would we feel
The sweet spell of love
And caress the
Dreams of emotion?
How would our great minds
Work hand-in-glove
Without tactile
Locomotion?

The love and genius of man
Depend on those beautiful hands.

Wilderness Hiking

"Can you see a puppy chasing a ball in the clouds above us?" Tricia asks as we lie on our backs in a meadow, miles from humanity. Thus begins a game that we repeat a million times. As we both get better at this, our skill at solving increasingly complex cloud-puzzles increases: "Do you see the Capricorn zodiac sign above the unicorn's head?"

The wilderness calls to us both as if we were avatars temporarily visiting a modern, urban world. We love the smells, the sounds—and the silence, the vistas, the night skies, the lakes and rivers, and, of course, all our breathing, sentient friends.

There is a sacred connection between us, at all times, but especially when we are in the wilderness. We are totally dependent upon each other, looking out for each other, alerting each other to the sights and wonders we are experiencing, sharing sacred moments, and merging our joyful hearts in the solitude. We both have a sacred connection with the earth and everything around us. There is no need for either of us to explain to the other how we feel, as we are both in the same place. God's hand is on our shoulder—we are one with the mystery that is called the Universe.

We collect rocks and sticks and feathers and turn them into works of art or ornaments. Some remain markers in the forest. Others we bring home. One day, we find a rock that is perfectly shaped like a heart, about the width of an outstretched hand. We place it against the base of a cedar tree that drapes over a river. We call this secret place "Heart Stone Rock," and we visit there in the wilderness almost every day, pausing to meditate and share prayers of gratitude for all the gifts that have been bestowed on us both—the greatest of which is each other.

One of the sweetest joys of our wilderness experience is being completely alone together. Each year, we embark on a two-week odyssey in Algonquin Park, a 7,000-square-kilometer wilderness preserve—larger than Belgium. There are no roads, electricity, Internet, or cell phone service. Access to the interior is only possible by kayak or canoe. The waters can be calm and beautiful—a shared joy; or they can be wild and stormy—an exhilarating adventure that we often survive together, and which always draws us closer.

Our love for Mother Earth and nature is only topped by our love for each other. Our love is a game we both play and we both always win—like when we play tennis together—because we never bother to keep score.

Sylvan Solace

Adder's-tongue beside coltsfoot,
The sultry perfume of dusk air,
Hedgerows proud with blackberry fruit,
Nature's gifts everywhere.

Open skies of red'ning hues
A "V" of geese—instinctive flight
Feed my senses and my soul
With inner calm and light.

Foal protected by her mare,
Last poppies of the summer sway.
Close by, a hidden vixen's lair
And castles made of hay.

A Love Story

Carpets crisp with rusting leaves
Beneath tombstones of fallen elm.
The Robin's scherzo, she believes
Commands the wooded realm.

Sinews feel the benefit
Of inclines leading to a view
Yielding a purer epithet
Than any words can ever do.

Yes, country walks can heal the breach
Between the Maker and the made.
Philosophy is what they teach
You in a country glade.

Water

*I*f there is one aspect of nature that calls more loudly to Tricia than any other, it is water—whether it is the ocean, a river, or a lake or pond. The sounds of water, the tastes and smells of water, the experience of being cradled by water, the adventure of water, and the embrace of the many temperaments of water connect to her watery soul. After all, she is the fixed water sign of Scorpio, which drives her need for security and causes her to reach for the deep in every person.

Water is like life. One doesn't fight, resist, or wrestle with water—if you do, you'll drown. Instead, we trust water, and give ourselves to it—and when we do, we float joyfully. As with water, so with life.

Tricia loves loons. They are among the most sacred animals of the northern wilderness, renowned for their haunting call. In the Native American or indigenous traditions, the loon symbolizes serenity, tranquility, and the reawakening of old hopes, wishes, and dreams. The loon is poorly adapted to the land, mostly relying on water, which is a symbol for dreams and multiple levels of consciousness. Loons, therefore, teach us to pay attention to our hopes, wishes, and dreams.

Loons love Tricia and me, too. Typically, loons travel in pairs, except when they are raising their families, seldom gathering in larger numbers. One day Tricia and I are traveling across the open water of Smoke Lake and are joined by a single loon. We pause to admire and pay our respects before moving on. As we do so, the solo loon follows our craft. Soon she is joined by another loon, and then another, until eventually 13 loons become pilots for our boat— a salute of mutual admiration.

On another occasion, I take a native drum in our canoe and I ask Trish to call out her heartbeat to me. As she does so, I begin drumming in unison with the rhythm she calls out, all the time bringing my own heartbeat into alignment with hers until we are entrained. As both our heartbeats share an identical rhythm with the drum, a loon appears beside our boat. Then another, and another, until 12 loons are following us. I've never heard anyone else from the north country share a similar experience. Tricia and I and the loons are in love.

Zen River

Steal away, my sons and daughters,
To the mountain streams and lakes,
To the land of rapid waters,
Where I learned about mistakes.

Gently launching, guide your craft out,
Paddle bravely from the shore.
Feel the sense of growing self-doubt
Weaken faith you had before.

Rushing waters grin and grasp you,
Steal your courage with a jeer.
Stretch and strain with every sinew—
Pitting power over fear.

Wrestle vainly with those rapids—
They will fight and cost you dear,
While her secret to your ear bids
If you're wise enough to hear.

Mighty River knows the wise way—
Just surrender to the flow
As she whispers to you gently,
"I'm your friend and not your foe."

Life is a river, smooth and tough—
Plenty of power to spare.
She gives you a choice: play with her rough,
Or seize her offer to share.

Morning Mist

The morning mist ascends to heaven
Carrying our prayers to the Great Spirit.
Thank you, Manitou, for your benediction,
As we love and laugh in the bosom of nature.

This rustic balm sparkles our souls—
The antidote for urban toxins.
In a brutish world that corrupts the Spirit,
Your summery beauty caresses and heals.

Can there be any gift as great
As the shared embrace of Nature and Lover?
The voice of the loon calls to the pines that reclaim
The mist as it settles. The healing continues.

The Rockies

*T*ricia and I met skiing. So it is only natural that we seek out skiing adventures and locations.

Tricia is a phenomenal skier, and it has taken me many years to match her skills. In fact, we've skied together so much, we ski almost identically now. Sometimes, just for fun, we even practice synchronized skiing together.

It isn't just the exhilaration of the sport, but, perhaps more importantly, it's the majesty and magic of the Rocky Mountains. No other location in the world (and I've skied just about everywhere) can equal the beauty, the quality of snow, the elevation, the scale, the lack of crowds, and the community of like-minded souls.

Tricia and I decide to spend half our year in the mountains. We build our new home from scratch and spend many years working with architects, builders, designers, furnishers, and scores of helpers and friends to create our dream mountain home. Eight years later, we buy another home further up the mountain and go through these rituals all over again. We keep our original home for our guests who participate in the retreats that Tricia and I run together.

When you arrive in the high country, you immediately experience a feeling of transformation. As Zora Neale Hurston wrote, "I have been in Sorrow's kitchen and licked out all the pots. Then I have stood on the peaky mountain wrapped in rainbows, with a harp and sword in my hands." The hustle and bustle of urban life, the cares of work, and all the irritations and frustrations of living fade away. Your boss looks really small from 12,500 feet! When all this vanishes, love remains.

Tricia's gifts with people are prodigious. Her ability to make our guests—anyone, actually—feel important, respected, and sacred is remarkable. She hosts complete strangers in our home with extraordinary elegance. Her sole purpose is to create a sensation of transcendence for guests. She makes them feel sacred and honored, lifts their hearts with her joyful nature, and ensures that they leave with their spirits higher than they were when they arrived.

You Are More

Observing the beauty around me
In the mountains of life where I grow,
One beauty alone does surround me
In ways that no other can know.

You are more than my day and my night
And the source of my dreams, I believe,
I need you from dawn until midnight,
Even more than the air I breathe.

Heaven's angels vamp with the tall peaks
As they dance to the blue skies above.
These seraphs and sierras are more when
Inspired by the power of our love.

Rituals

*A*mong the secrets of our love affair, we discover, are the many rituals we have created for us both to enjoy: a daily hike in the woods, sleeping in, then sipping cappuccinos in bed on Sunday mornings, watching the sun set with a "sundowner," floating on a mattress in the swimming pool while we massage each other's feet, watching the annual Perseid meteor shower, making angels in the snow, or blowing dandelion seeds into the wind.

On one of my business trips, I discover a very interesting item called "Cross-My-Heart-Stones." Each one is about the size of a quarter. They are semiprecious stones made from chiastolite, a variety of andaludite, that have a natural cross that runs throughout each one, and the stones themselves have been shaped into a three-dimensional heart. I bring them home and give one to Tricia and keep one for myself. From that day forward, Tricia and I are always connected by, among many other things, our Cross-My-Heart-Stones—one in my pocket, wherever I am, and the other with Tricia, wherever she is.

Our Canadian home is built on the edge of a cliff, which overlooks a large flat, open area. Each winter, I put on my snowshoes and trek down there to create a giant heart—a message of love to Tricia—which radiates from the valley floor every time she passes the window. When snow falls, I rework the outline to keep its message bright.

Before we begin to live together, Tricia and I send each other many cards, a tradition we have continued ever since. Each is an expression of our love for each other. Over time, we accumulate many hundreds of them, each with unique phrasings describing the depths of our commitment, passion, love, and respect. Over the years, as we move our homes, our very large collection of cards becomes a significant chattel. Eventually, we both turn this into a game. When I travel, I write a card before I leave, and then hide it somewhere where I think she will find it—under the cream in the fridge, where it will be visible when she makes her morning coffee; behind her shampoo, where it will be discovered during her morning shower; under her bed clothes, where her toes will discover it when she retires for the evening.

Tricia's espionage work is more of a challenge than mine—there's really only one place you can hide my card when I'm traveling and that's in my carry-on luggage. Sometimes she hides it in a shirt, other times in my toilet bag, or in a client file—and if I accidentally discover it before I leave, I pretend that I have not done so, to keep the game alive.

The joy that these rituals generate is so sweet that I glow all day after discovering my card, which I do as soon as I arrive at my hotel, having held myself in suspense until I can tear apart my bag and find this little treasure in the privacy of my new, temporary home. I know she will do the same, and in our evening phone call, we will share our stories—where we were when we discovered our cards, how they made us laugh, the joy we both experienced, and how they inspired our day. These little rituals are the enhancer of the joy in our lives. To quote Pablo Neruda, "To feel the love of people whom we love is a fire that feeds our life."

My Joy

If I should pass from this great hall
Into the fields of bliss,
No joy will equal that I shared
With you with every kiss.

If banished be my candle bright
To where no man has seen,
My guiding star will be that blaze
Of joy that you have been.

And if my ashen world should yield
No Phoenix to arise,
My strength and joy will come from deep
Within your loving eyes.

Singing and Dancing

Music is a kind of emotional glue that connects
Tricia and me in ethereal ways. She pays
careful attention to the lyrics and their
hidden meaning, and she does this much better than
I do; I am more interested in the melody and the musicianship of the players, and we both teach each other,
from these different perspectives, what we are hearing
and experiencing, and thus, our musical experience
becomes so much greater. We are forever introducing
each other to new artists, new music, and new musical
experiences.

Tricia loves to dance, too, and when one of her
favorite songs fills the air, her feet (a tiny size six) carry
her away. I hope for her to dance me to the end of love.[2]

[2]From a lyric by Leonard Cohen, "Dance Me to the End of Love"
(http://www.lyricsoverload.com/lyrics/Leonard-Cohen-
Dance-Me-to-the-End-of-Love-lyrics/71178)

As Josh Turner, one of Tricia's favorite artists, has put it:

> *So baby, why don't we just dance*
> *Down the hall,*
> *Maybe straight up the stairs?*
> *Bouncing off the wall,*
> *Floating on air,*
> *Baby, why don't we just dance?*

Another song that we love is called "Tshinanu," by the native group Kashtin. It is a very catchy number, and has a solid melody, but an unusual tempo, making it strangely difficult to dance to. As a result, Tricia and I make up our own dance to this song, which we name "The Pee Dance" because the only dancing move that seems to fit the rhythm is a gyration one might expect from a human with a full bladder. Every time we do this dance, we laugh so hard that we collapse, unable to finish the dance.

But laughter is a dance too. It is said that Socrates learned to dance when he was seventy because he felt that an essential part of himself had been neglected.

Dancing—at least the way Tricia and I do it, is our blissful connection to the Universe, an uncensored expression of our joy and zest for life. Kurt Vonnegut said, "Dance, even if you have nowhere to do it but your living room"—and we do, almost every day. When we dance together—in the kitchen, in the hall, in our bedroom, or in a honky-tonk in Rifle, Colorado, or a Western tavern in Copper Mountain, or a beach in Jamaica—it is a shortcut to happiness. As Friedrich Nietzsche said, "I would believe only in a God that knows how to dance." He also said, "We should consider every day lost on which we have not danced at least once." We haven't missed many days—four feet, two hearts, one luscious moment—daily.

The Dancer and the Dance

The dance and the dancer are one
Becoming the knower and the known;
Countless octaves pour from the heart
In a symphony of wild aliveness.

Dance the Creator's fandango
Two hearts entwined in a riff of glee,
Dreaming together with our feet
Expressing gratitude for the present.

Her body tells the naked truth
She is in love with the Universe,
Clasping it tightly to her chest
A sweet, sinewy athlete of God.

A Love Story

The hidden language of the soul
Joyfully shouts, "You are the dancer—
Each blessed step of Life's the dance."
As you sashay and spin, the World stands still.

Such carefree joy blesses my heart
As she dances right out of herself.
No one has danced this dance before.
In this moment, no other world exists.

Eloping

*T*ricia and I have lived together for nine years. We have discussed marrying, but we notice that many of our friends who had lived together and then married, suddenly found their relationship in jeopardy. We are so madly in love that we decide we will not jeopardize our love story by marrying. A paradox.

But I know her mom would be over-the-moon to see us married. Tricia's mom loves us unconditionally, and nothing makes her happier in her entire life than the knowledge that her daughter is so deeply in love and cared for. Even so, she is old-school, and so I secretly plot a wedding. I tried to arrange a secret wedding once before, a couple of years ago, in a magical location called Pecos River, New Mexico. At the time, we were conducting high-event learning experiences—climbing-walls, zip lines, and jumping off telephone poles. I had planned to propose to Tricia from the top of a 60-foot pole prior to jumping off it, but, at the last minute, our event was canceled, and so I aborted the romantic ruse.

But a new opportunity has presented itself—I have an assignment in Bermuda. So, unbeknownst to Tricia, I work closely with a local wedding coordinator to arrange our wedding. He very efficiently (and secretly) handles all the paperwork, books a romantic setting for our ceremony (a cliff-top overlooking a coral-pink beach at Astwood Cove), complete with a Bermuda-shorts-clad minister, and he also plays the role of videographer while his wife takes the photographs. Six weeks before we leave for this trip, a complication occurs: a skiing accident shatters my leg in nine places.

So I need to cook up some blarney to persuade Tricia to accompany me to Bermuda because I am hobbling about in crutches and, um, need someone to carry my bags, computer, and projection equipment that I will use in my speech.

Tricia innocently inquires about a dress code. I suggest that, er, since there will likely be a cocktail reception, it would be wise for her to pack an appropriate dress. She first selects a blue one. I shake my head, dismissing it with some feeble decoy reasoning. Then she shows me a yellow one, which I similarly turn down. Finally, she picks out a white dress. I smile privately to myself and say, "Perfect!"

After arriving in Bermuda, we jump into a cab and head for dinner. As we settle into the back seats, I ask the driver to insert music I have prerecorded into the player in his dashboard. It contains all our favorite love songs. As the music plays, I ask Tricia,

"Will you marry me?"

"Oh no! We have already agreed that people who live together, and then marry, end up with crashed relationships."

"No," I say, getting a little nervous now. "Really. Will you marry me?"

"Of course! When would you like to get married?"

"The day after tomorrow!"

Tricia gulps, then the radiance on her face grows like the molten lava from a volcano—it could keep a big city warm for months.

We have a delicious dinner at a restaurant called "Once Upon a Table," where the owners make a big fuss of their two lovebird guests. We spend the next day on a pink beach, where we write our wedding vows together. The following day at 4:30 p.m., a horse-drawn hackney carriage escorts us serenely, like a royal couple, from our hotel to Astwood Cove, a gorgeous cliff-top location overlooking the pink beach and the azure ocean. We are married by a local minister, who asks if anyone has any reason to challenge our union, but no one in the growing throng of tourists demurs. They are more concerned with taking pictures. When the minister asks for the wedding rings, I reveal them, like a rabbit from a hat—I have had them secretly designed and made weeks before, and hidden them in our luggage.

The next day, I address a conference of 3,000 people, and many in the audience nudge each other and, pointing, whisper, "That's the guy that we saw getting married on the top of the cliff!" The next week, the headlines in the business section of the June 3, 1993, edition of Bermuda's *The Royal Gazette* proclaim, "Author's Love Story Ends with Surprise Bermuda Wedding."

Our Wedding Vows

I want you to know that I love you,
And I will for the rest of my days.
I will trust and respect you,
Tell the truth and embrace you.
Every day. All the time. And always.

For the rest of our lives together,
Every day in your favor I'll bend.
I'll make rain seem like dew—
I'll make you smile when you're blue.
That's forever and ever. Amen.

A New Home

I am deliriously happy. Life is perfect. Our commute is a twenty-second dance with our wonder dog, Spirit, from the master bedroom to our respective offices. Our setting is so stunning that our employees take photographs of their work environment, the swimming pool, the deer foraging in the gardens, the hummingbirds at their feeders, our canoe and snow-shoes hanging on the building's exterior, and of course the spectacular views. They send these to their friends with pride—"This is my office!"

But we have grown, and twelve employees are now showing up every day, causing Tricia and me to retreat to the one room in our house not yet converted into office space—our bedroom. All the other bedrooms have become the personal workspaces of our team members, and, grateful though we are for our commercial success, we feel like 9-to-5 prisoners. Even in the evenings, the house is not really a home because it is cluttered with computers, telephones, and the other office paraphernalia necessary to conduct a global business.

Below the cliffs on which our house is perched, freshwater springs flow out of the many fissures there, tinkling their joyful symphony. We have built a 40-foot deck cantilevered over the edge, which we call our "morning deck" because the sunrise embraces it, enfolding us in its golden endearment. It is here that Tricia and I contemplate life, the world, and our dreams.

We know that we need to find a larger home. Our neighbor owns a home that is larger than ours—a vintage cottage to which he has added upgrades and additions over the years. After the contractors go home, Tricia and I sneak through the woods to inspect their work, so we know the bones of this house are sound.

I suggest to Tricia that she should take her beautiful brown eyes over to our neighbor and charm him into selling his newly remodeled home. She does so, but is rebuffed. And so we continue to live in our cramped quarters, but loving it. Two years later, sitting on our morning deck, Tricia and I agree that she should try again. This time she is successful, and we agree to the vendor's terms and move into our new home. Our old love nest becomes our corporate headquarters, and we gratefully settle into our new love nest.

This is Tricia's dream home. Our daily commute is no longer 20 seconds down the hall, but a 60-second journey through a trail in the woods that separates our new home from our log cabin office. Our new home is peaceful, joyful, and the cradle of love. The most joyful sound to my ears is the carillon of Tricia's songs as she sings blissfully for herself. She has a beautiful voice and can carry a tune, and that in itself is a blessing. But the greater gift is my sense that I have helped to create a life for us both that makes her so happy, her heart sings— and therefore mine does, too.

Two Souls—One Flame

If you have never loved another so deeply

That you poured the entire contents of
your soul into theirs,

And if you have never been loved by someone
who poured the entire contents
of their soul into yours,

Then you have not yet lived life as it was ordained.

Love is life; if you haven't loved, you haven't lived.

Travel

I miss Trish (she goes by Tricia and Trish) so much when I travel that I call her four or five times a day. I am conscious of being a frequent flyer and I know that there are over 100 crashes every year, so I always call Tricia just before I get on the airplane. I'm hedging my bets—if I'm going to die, then Tricia's voice will be singing in my ears as we dive into the ocean, and Tricia will have the memory of my voice, too.

I am not afraid of dying. I am afraid that my last words to Tricia might not be, "I love you." One can die at any moment, and so I reason that it is best to live, not as if this might be our last day, but rather, as though it is *the only, and the best, day.*

I call when I land, so that Tricia knows I'm safe, and because I love the symphony of her laugh (and I can always make her laugh!). I call for good luck before I make a speech, and I call right afterward to let her know how it went. I nearly always call before I go to bed. If Tricia hasn't mentioned the love card that I always hide for her somewhere, then I assume she has not yet discovered it, and so I will call her to offer a subtle clue.

Apart

I miss the caress of your cheek on my chest
As my fingers comb through your hair,
But more than this, what I really miss
Is the joy of your just being there.

I love the caress of your voice in my heart
Our souls dancing perfectly us—
Nobody's there, as we declare
A million shades of amorous.

I miss the embrace of the love in your mind
And sweet nothings during the night;
No amount of miles can erase my smiles
When I dream of holding you tight.

And I Think of You

Cones carpet the forest floor...
I smile, and I think of you.

Glacier waters spill over the Bow Falls...
I smile, and I think of you.

Rushing snowmelt scours the valley...
I smile, and I think of you.

I stroke the crusted redwood bark...
I smile, and I think of you.

Two finches tease me with their love song...
I smile, and I think of you.

Pebbles skip over the river of life...
I smile, and I think of you.

The river's melody plays in my ears...
I smile, and I think of you.

I'm drugged with the Rocky Mountain high...
I smile and I think of you.

Nature's chorus fills my soul...
I smile, and I think of you.

The seasons change and bring me peace...
I smile, and I think of you.

The trickster soars and shoots the moon...
I smile, and I think of you.

I thank the Source for the gift of life...
I smile, and I think of you.

A Mischievous Mink

*T*ricia often comes to meet me at the airport when I return from my frequent business travels. After landing one very cold winter evening, I deplane and emerge into the airport terminal. Among the many greeters, I see Trish standing elegantly, as she always does, but this time, in a full-length mink coat.[3]

Although I've only been away for 48 hours, we greet as if it's been 48 years. I slip my hand inside her mink coat to hold her more closely, and I am stunned—there are no clothes underneath her fur!

I hurry this mischievous creature out of the terminal building and into our car, whistling her home safely, but rapidly.

The rest of the story is censored.

[3] This was years ago, when it was the practice of Mary Kay to reward top sales directors with a full-length mink coat. For the benefit of the environmentally conscious reader: the company has since discontinued this practice, and we no longer support the wearing of fashion furs.

The Gifts I See
When You Go Away

Priceless treasures from your heart,
And rainbows from your mind
More clearly seen when we're apart
For the one who's left behind.
I see them when you are here,
And treasure all you do,
But when you are no longer near,
I love those sweet gifts anew.

When two lovers are so close,
It's easy to ignore
The things that mean the very most—
These sweet treasures I adore.
Like a squirrel in a cage
I get as blind as can be
Forgetting to pay homage
For the gifts you give to me.

The puzzling thing for me
Is that I more clearly see
The gifts you give so freely
When you are away from me.

You'd entrust your very soul
Needing nothing from me;
Your absence makes a sacred hole
And I prize your gifts to me.
Is everyone else like me
When two souls are as one?
Are you finding that you can see
Those gifts better when alone?

Spirit

*S*pirit, the name we give our wonder dog, a Hungarian Vizsla, is born five days before we are married. She will bless our lives for 14 years. More than that, she will become an international star.

Over the years, Spirit will become our most important teacher. She gives us lessons that we strive to weave into our daily lives. We use her lessons to teach others. One day, the American Veterinary Medical Association invites me to be the keynote speaker at their annual convention. I tell them that we have an amazing team member called Spirit, and we would like to bring her with us. Tricia and I take Spirit to the city, which she has never seen before, and it represents a million treats for her. The conference organizers have built a little kennel on stage with her name above it, and Tricia takes her place in the front row of the auditorium with Spirit on her lap. I make my speech, and as I conclude, the MC approaches the stage to thank me. Spirit is wriggling, desperately wanting to leap from the audience onto the stage, and Tricia is unable to restrain her. Spirit bounds up onto the stage, leaps into my arms and immediately starts to lick my head. Three thousand people in the audience rise to their feet to offer a standing ovation!

Spirit taught us a great deal. Here are some of the lessons:

Every day is new day—don't dwell on the past.

Be happy.

Love what you do so much that there is no difference between Monday and Saturday.

Run, romp, and play daily.

Experience the pure ecstasy of fresh air and the wind in your face.

Leave room in your schedule for regular naps and stretch before rising.

If you are uncomfortable, just go to another place that feels better.

If it itches, scratch it.

Give people lots of attention and welcome their
affection.

Be tactile—welcome strokes.

Practice vulnerability, humility, and obedience—it
is usually in your best interests.

Be kind, no matter what others do.

Always be ready to learn something new. The
rewards can be handsome.

When it feels right, make lots of noise.

Forgiveness is a wonderful thing—don't hold
grudges for more than two minutes.

Harbor no hidden agendas.

No matter how often you are scolded, don't buy
into the guilt thing and pout…run right back
and make friends. Hold no rancor.

When someone is unwell, sit beside them and
comfort them. Comfort your friends. No
matter what happens, be there.

Be loyal.

If you ever feel angry, remember these three words of advice: get over it.

If what you want what lies buried, dig until you find it.

Remember the Law of Dog Karma: What you give is what you get.

Your personal mission should be: "To be the kind of person my dog thinks I am."

Spirit (there is a good reason why we call her "Spirit, the wonder dog"!) reminds us to be humble and to be one with nature... I wrote the following poem one day when I was sitting on top of a hill looking into the bush in South Africa (where it is called the *veld*). The plateau, which seemed to stretch for hundreds of miles, shimmered in the searing heat of the noonday sun. I imagined that it was filled with creatures much smarter than me—I was sitting in the scorching heat, and they had taken shelter in the veld...

The Lowveld Lesson

High noon; silent was the veld
But hearkening ears were cocked
As their forms in the bush did melt
And they watched me and they mocked.

Nature is at war with man
As he seeks to comprehend
The biodynamic plan
That was meant to have no end.

Leopard, Cheetah and Kudu,
Please pledge that you won't despair;
Man learns more slowly than you,
But soon he will learn to care.

For man will discern your truth
And listen to what you say.
Nature lays claim to us both;
It's brilliantly planned that way.

On Building a Deep, Abiding Relationship

*T*ricia and I marvel at the magic of our relationship and conclude that we should share it with the world. So we sit down and write a list of all the things we can think of that have made, and continue to make, our relationship so special:

Regularly ask, "How may I serve you?"

Each of us has a life—three degrees—yours, mine, and ours.

The total truth prevails—always.

No secrets (about anything)—we are one.

Always look into the eyes of your partner.

Touch tenderly and frequently.

Say, "I love you" daily—or more often.

Trust beyond reason, and assume the best.

Be loyal without question.

Pay attention to each other.

Don't take happiness for granted.

Take time together—respect the power and sacredness of place.

Agree wherever you can; contradict as little as possible.

Disagreements (not arguments) have a daylight-only shelf-life.

Identify, and then live into, your shared dream.

Be each other's number one best friend—as well as lovers and partners.

Learn to say, "I'm sorry."

Forgive.

Dare to be vulnerable and to reveal yourself.

Be inventively playful and invest in fun.

Have romantic and playful rituals—like cards (see "Rituals").

Find ways to keep your relationship fresh.

My Love for You

*To the fire of the Koh-i-noor gem
Add the crash of Niagara's power,
The bouquet of Chateau d'Ychem
And the wonder of Eiffel's Tower:
They're less than my love for you.*

*All the joy of Ravel's Bolero
And the prose of Shakespeare and Milton,
The distinction of each flake of snow
And the dreams that visions are built on,
Can't equal my love for you.*

*Not even Tennyson or Thoreau,
Nor Chopin or Mozart or Brahms,
Or all the poets of tomorrow
Could tell you in a million psalms,
The depth of my love for you.*

Storm Clouds

y soul-brother, Moe Dixon, entertains crowds of up to 500 with his singing, in a rowdy Western tavern called JJ's. He is an extraordinarily talented musician and plays many stringed instruments, including the guitar and ukulele. Tricia and I go there regularly to listen to him and enjoy his music, to dance, and to visit with all our friends who come to this place regularly. It is a center of happiness. Over the years, we spend countless evenings here. During the ski season, there are many festive events that become celebratory rituals—Christmas Day, New Year's Eve, Mardi Gras, St. Patrick's Day—the house is always packed and each one of these is a festive event to remember. Moe has learned the special songs that Tricia loves, and he plays them for her as soon as he sees her walking in the door.

At JJ's, there is a long bar—perhaps 35 feet in length. It is lined with stools upon which are seated many partygoers enjoying an after-ski-day beverage. The Tiffany lamps sway erratically over their heads in unison with the rowdy environment. Standing on top of the bar, Tricia is gyrating, her face disguised with a feathered Mardi Gras mask, an inflatable guitar in her hands, lip-syncing to Moe's music, having the time of her life with her audience, from whom she elicits raucous cheers. She is in a blissful trance in a place, and with people, she loves.

I am not there. I am in the town's business office receiving a fax. It is Tricia's histopathology report. My heart falls out of my stomach. The cancer that Tricia has been fighting for so many years has metastasized and reached across her beautiful body. I'm on my knees, which have crumpled as the wind has been knocked out of me. I am hyperventilating and I can't control my howling.

I wait until I can muster at least a nominal amount of composure. Rising to my feet, I begin the longest walk of my life—the journey to JJ's to tell Tricia the news that she never wanted to hear.

Be Gone, Dark Angel

The rhythm of life, so ordered and clear,
Till the Dark Angel brings a message of fear.
"Dark One, what is it you wish me to learn?"
"The choice is yours; only you can discern."
My planet is rocked; my head is unclear.
And first I retreat to a place of despair.
But then my soul says, "I decline this call,
I'm outta here. Good-bye, y'all."
What's delivered to me I need not take,
I am the king of my soul; lord of my fate.
My partner for life takes orders from none
She will triumph, Dark Angel—so get you gone!

Home Movies

The camera in my head
Plays old movies starring you
I play them every night
In the daytime too
Frame by frame
Between live performances.

I Love You Like Crazy

*E*ven as Tricia declines, her pixie dust is ever-present below the surface, frequently emerging in gratitude or in playful ways. Even in these twilight days, she frequently comments about how happy she is, our closeness, and the good times we are having together.

Still, she can spread her pixie dust—somehow, she finds the energy to locate a card and hide it under my pillow. On the outside it says, "Wild Thing" and inside it says, "I think I love you!", but she has crossed out "think" and replaced it with "KNOW." In her writing, which has become weak now, she pens these precious words: "Dearest Leo Love (I am a Leo), you have been an amazing nurse, friend, mentor, companion, chauffeur, empath, and guide. Thank you, Love, for your patience, humor, understanding, discipline, friendship, and love. I love you like crazy!"

I have been at Tricia's side for a year now. In these last days, we make arrangements to transfer her to a hospice, but on the day she is scheduled to be transferred, I can't do it. As Tricia's spirit prepares to depart, I can feel her tearing away from my heart. I love her so totally, even more than ever, and I want to be with her and serve her. I am not naturally drawn to patient care or dealing with sickness, but I realize that in these last moments of her earthly journey (what Tricia called Earth School) she is giving me the greatest gift—the opportunity to serve unconditionally, from the heart—for the rest of her life. It is a gift I selfishly want for myself, and I cancel her transfer to the hospice.

Tricia can't speak anymore, but she squeezes my hand three times—it's the secret way we have told each other, "I love you" when words were not practical.

I hold Tricia's hand as she releases her last breath and her beautiful spirit soars from our paradise to an even greater one.

For Whom Is It You're Weeping?

For whom is it you're weeping
Down there beside the cist?
Is it "God-Speed" you're saying
As swirls of grief persist?
Are they tears of joy for knowing
Her pains will now desist
Or of anguish as you're thinking
How daily she'll be missed?

For whom is it you're weeping
As you make farewells today?
Did you run out of seasons,
With still so much to say?
Can all the wasted chances
By tears be washed away?
Would plans be all completed
Had there just been one more day?

For whom is it you're weeping
The living or the sleeping?

Goodbye

*I*t is my beloved Tricia's birthday. She would be 61.
We are holding this Celebration of her Life today,
and it is a magnificent affair. It is being held at the
West Lodge of the members-only Caledon Ski Club, a
hundred yards from the exact spot on the ski hill where
we met 30 years ago, when she fell and I helped her to
her feet and blew the snow out of her ear. There are
flowers everywhere, a first-class caterer is doing a
marvelous job of feeding everyone, a slideshow is
projecting on a big screen showing more than a hundred
pictures of Tricia and her rich life, and over one hundred
of Tricia's favorite songs are playing through the sound
system. The room is surrounded with Tricia's paintings
and other art, such as our wedding vows, and other
expressions of her brilliance and our devotion.

The Celebration begins with a native healing ceremony conducted by a native shaman, Gord Theo. He
smokes the Pipe of Peace, and then passes it to me to
smoke on behalf of everyone, both present and absent.
Then Larry Kurtz, a renowned blues singer and
harmonica player, plays some wonderful songs and talks
about his relationship with Tricia. Then I speak for a
while, telling stories that few have heard before, illus-
trating the intimate closeness that Tricia and I enjoyed,
and our amazing love affair. I invite everyone to play
musical chairs: I ask each person to choose a partner. As I
tell a story around a particular song, I explain why it was
so important to us, before playing a short segment of that
song as everybody rocks with their partner. I ask everyone
to change partners while I tell the story behind another
song, before playing it as they dance with a new partner.
We do this seven times. A spirit of joy pervades the gathering. As everyone catches their breath, several friends and
family members share moving stories about how Tricia
touched, and in many cases changed, their lives. Mean-
while, Mark Grice, Tricia's art teacher, is painting a canvas
depicting the backcountry areas in which Tricia and I

hiked, and then he offers his freshly painted canvas for auction in aid of a charity called the Bruce Trail Conservancy, which manages the trails that Tricia and I hiked almost every day. Moe Dixon, my soul-brother from JJ's and the number-one après ski entertainer in America, follows by getting everybody hopping and crying, as he plays a half dozen of Tricia's favorite "Moe tunes." The excitement builds as Doug Sole, a world-famous drummer and drum circle leader, engages the entire group in a Nigerian traditional peace song, followed by a drum circle (he has brought 30 drums). Those who do not have a drum receive one or another form of percussion instrument to play. It is a marvelous crescendo to the afternoon, capped with a champagne toast.

I have asked everyone to bring their dancing shoes, and as the proceedings unfold, they soon understand why. This is not an "Amazing Grace" kind of experience, because Trish would not have wanted that. It is a *party*, and everyone is leaving with a smile on their faces, having experienced the kind of lightness and a sprinkling of the pixie dust that Tricia shared with everyone with whom she connected.

Tricia is teaching them how to REALLY dance up there now!

One early morning, a month after the Celebration of Tricia's Life, I am following Tricia's and my daily routine—sitting in our hot tub nursing my coffee. But now, I am alone, so I am meditating and also crying as I nurse my pain. Through my tears, I wonder, "Where are you, Trish?"—a question I ask a lot these days. I am crying with complete abandon as there is no one in this wilderness to hear me except Tricia. As the sun rises from below the horizon, I marvel at its beauty. I think about how much Trish loved sunrises, and I realize that it must be Trish, and that everything that is beautiful is Trish—she's everywhere. As C. S. Lewis wrote, "He had ceased to be in particular places in order to meet us everywhere." Even my nickname for Tricia was "Beautiful." It was the message I had been waiting for. I wrote this poem immediately that morning—it recalls many of her favorite moments—it's beautiful, so "It Must Be You."

It Must Be You

The call of the loon,
The alpenglow,
The eclipse of the moon—
They're beautiful:
So they must be you.

The double rainbow,
The mist in the vale,
The silent snow—
They're beautiful:
So they must be you.

A puppy's love,
Sunset and Merlot,
The clouds above—
They're beautiful:
So they must be you.

These favorite moments
Of magic and joy
(Here at least)
They're beautiful:
So they must be you.

They say that God's in everything:
The dances we share
And the songs we sing—
They're beautiful:
So they must be you.

I searched for you—
Looked everywhere.
And then I knew,
Everything's beautiful:
Because it's you.

A Message from Trish

I've recited our wedding vows almost every day over the last 30 years. I've tried almost every day, not always successfully, to live them too. Tricia and I both did. It was the secret, and the magic, of our divine harmony. *(Read the vows on page 71.)* We loved with a love that was even deeper than love.

Three months after Trish died, a friend asked me if I would perform a wedding ceremony for her daughter and her soon-to-be husband. I had never conducted a wedding ceremony before, so I needed to get up to speed in numerous ways. I spoke to the bride and told her about Tricia. I explained that if her upcoming marriage would be half as successful as ours had been, then she and her love would both be in heaven.

I asked the bride-to-be if she and her love had written their own vows yet and she said they had not.

I offered to give her Tricia's and my wedding vows, because they are so inherently beautiful and carry the powerful karma of our 30-year love story. The opportunity to share this gift with a young couple as deeply in love as we had been, since before they were both born, was an opportunity to pay it forward, and create a beautiful legacy from Tricia and me.

About a month later, I was reciting our wedding vows in my usual way, affirming my commitment to Tricia—from my mortal plane to her ethereal one. The words, "For the rest of our lives together..." didn't seem to ring quite true. And, "I'll make you smile when you're blue" is redundant for someone who keeps company with angels—she is forever smiling now—no need for any help from me!

Suddenly, I received a message: the vows, which are mutual, no longer spoke appropriately to Tricia's and my new relationship. Tricia wanted to give me new words, a new message, taking our wedding vows, made so many years ago, and adapting them to our new reality.

Honore de Balzac wrote, "A woman knows the face of the man she loves as a sailor knows the open sea."

This is what Tricia whispered to me from her celestial domain to my earthly one...

Tricia's Message[4]

I want you to know that I love you,
Even more than our earlier days.
I will love and protect you,
Hold your hand and embrace you,
Every day. All the time. And always.

The rest of our lives are as one,
Every day both our heartbeats will blend;
I'll make rain seem like dew—
I'll make you smile when you're blue.
That's forever and ever. Amen.

> *Love has no age,*
> *no limit; and no death.*
>
> —John Galsworthy

---

[4] You can compare this message to our original
weddings vows, which are on page 71.

Other Books by Lance Secretan

The Spark, the Flame, and the Torch:
Inspire Self. Inspire Others. Inspire the World.

ONE: The Art and Practice of Conscious Leadership

Inspire! What Great Leaders Do

Spirit@Work: Bringing Spirit and Values to Work

Inspirational Leadership: Destiny, Calling and Cause

Reclaiming Higher Ground:
Creating Organizations That Inspire the Soul

Living the Moment: A Sacred Journey

The Way of the Tiger:
Gentle Wisdom for Turbulent Times

The Masterclass: Modern Fables for Working and Living

Managerial Moxie:
The 8 Proven Steps to Empowering Employees and
Supercharging Your Company

CDs by Lance Secretan

The Spark, the Flame, and the Torch:
The Journey to Higher Ground Leadership®

ONE: The Art and Practice of Conscious Leadership

Inspire! What Great Leaders Do

Inspirational Leadership®: Destiny, Calling and Cause